WORLD'S BEST
LIFE HACKS

200
INGENIOUS WAYS TO USE
EVERYDAY OBJECTS

BY SARAH DEVOS

weldon**owen**

WHAT ARE LIFE HACKS? THEY'RE SMART, "GEE, I NEVER WOULD HAVE THOUGHT OF THAT!" SOLUTIONS TO ALL OF LIFE'S DAILY DILEMMAS.

They're those little tricks that keep you one step ahead of life—ways to use ordinary items for a different purpose, or to transform an object into something entirely new beyond its intended purpose. Or they can just be quick little tips that help you save time, effort, or money. Why make it hard when it can be easy?

The term originates in the computer world: A hack is a small program or practical solution to solve a problem. And a life hack is just that, except it's no longer limited to your laptop. These days, there's a life hack for every small area of your life, as you'll soon see!

So where did all these ideas come from? I made a list of the best hacks I know, dug up my mom's wise tips, scoured the Internet and sifted through books, and knocked on friends' and neighbors' doors. I had one single goal: to collect 200 original, useful life hacks.

One by one I tried them out, with the help of a few friends. If one hack wasn't good enough, it instantly flew off the Holy List of Life Hacks. Eucalyptus in your shower for a nice sauna scent? Nope, it doesn't work. A hollowed-out orange half makes a candle? Not a chance.

Some tips you probably already knew. Some you may have forgotten. Who knows, some may blow your mind. So simple, yet so smart! Anyhow, the 200 life hacks in this book really work.

Whether you read this list because you are frugal, lazy, inventive, environmentally conscious, or simply curious, if you have this book your life will never be the same!

I wish you much pleasure in reading and trying these out!

SARAH

DOES YOUR GIFT WRAP UNROLL? CUT AN EMPTY TOILET PAPER TUBE
AND SLIDE IT ON THE GIFT-WRAP ROLL TO KEEP THE PAPER IN PLACE.

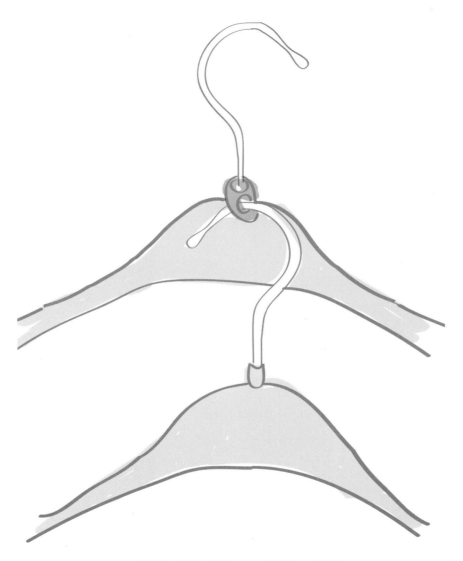

SODA CAN TAB = DOUBLE SPACE!

MOVING? PAPER PLATES BETWEEN YOUR SO-CALLED REAL PLATES
WILL SAVE YOU A TON OF NEWSPAPER!

VACUUM CLEANER SMELLS STALE? TRY VACUUMING UP A LITTLE LAUNDRY SOAP.

BELIEVE IT OR NOT, A SQUEAKY DOOR WILL STOP ITS SQUEAKING IF YOU SLIGHTLY LIFT THE DOOR WHILE YOU OPEN IT (OR IF YOU GREASE THE HINGES, OF COURSE).

YOU CAN POUR COFFEE GROUNDS DOWN YOUR KITCHEN SINK
TO KEEP YOUR DRAINS NICE AND CLEAN.

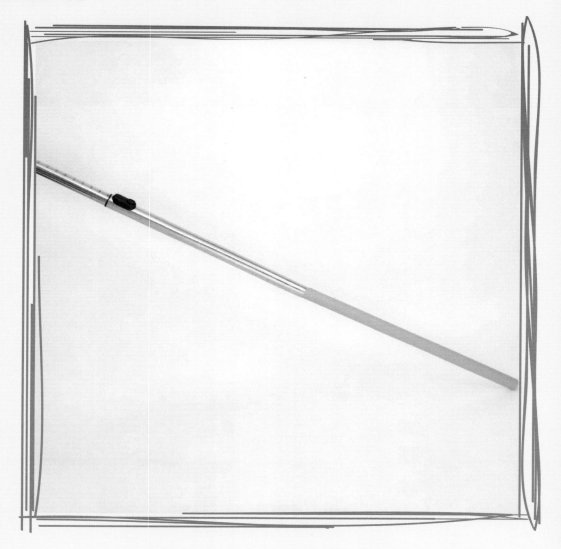

GIFT WRAP ALL USED UP? PUT THAT CARDBOARD TUBE TO GOOD USE AS AN EXTENSION ARM FOR YOUR VACUUM CLEANER.

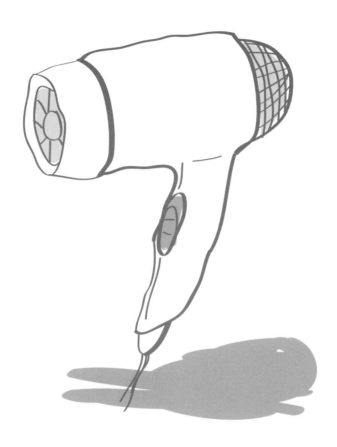

WANT TO SPEED-DEFROST YOUR FREEZER? UNPLUG IT, PUT DOWN SOME
TOWELS, AND SET YOUR BLOW-DRYER ON LOW HEAT...THEN BLAST THAT
ICE AWAY! (NEVER PUT THE BLOW-DRYER ON A WET SURFACE.)

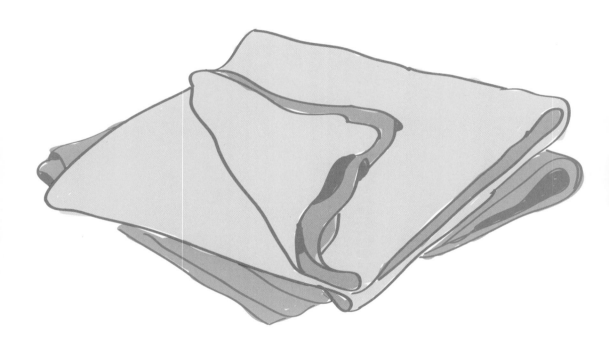

WHO SAID YOU NEED SOAP AND WATER TO WASH WINDOWS?
HOORAY FOR MICROFIBER CLOTHS!

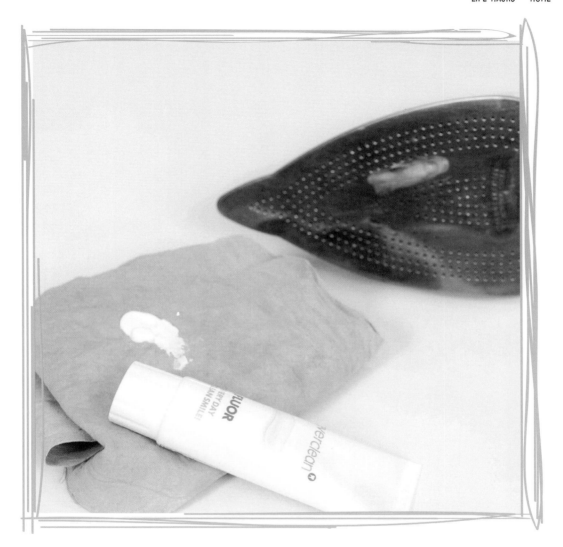

SPREAD A LITTLE TOOTHPASTE ON A CHAMOIS CLOTH AND RUB IT ON
THE SOLE OF YOUR IRON (JUST KEEP IT OUT OF THE SMALL HOLES).
LET SIT FOR A FEW MINUTES, THEN WIPE CLEAN. BLING BLING!

ATTACH YOUR SOCKS IN PAIRS BEFORE THROWING THEM IN THE WASH.
BYE BYE, LONELY SOCKS!

LOST AN EARRING SOMEWHERE AT HOME? PULL AN OLD NYLON SOCK OR
A PAIR OF PANTYHOSE OVER YOUR VACUUM CLEANER'S NOZZLE AND GIVE
YOUR PLACE A GOOD ONCE-OVER. YOU'LL FIND THAT EARRING QUICKLY!

WHO DOESN'T LOVE A LITTLE LIGHT BATHROOM READING?
GIVE THOSE CHEAP HANGERS AND MAGAZINES LYING
AROUND YOUR HOUSE A COMMUNAL PURPOSE.

CUTTING A SLIT IN A WINE CORK TO SEAL A BAG OF CHIPS =
A GREAT EXCUSE FOR OPENING A BOTTLE OF GOOD WINE!

GLUE RESIDUE ON JARS—EVEN THE STUBBORN STUFF THAT RESISTS
THE DISHWASHER—WILL DISAPPEAR WHEN TREATED WITH A MIX OF
WASHING SODA AND VEGETABLE OIL. LET IT SIT FOR 15 MINUTES,
SCRUB, AND RINSE FOR A SQUEAKY-CLEAN JAR!

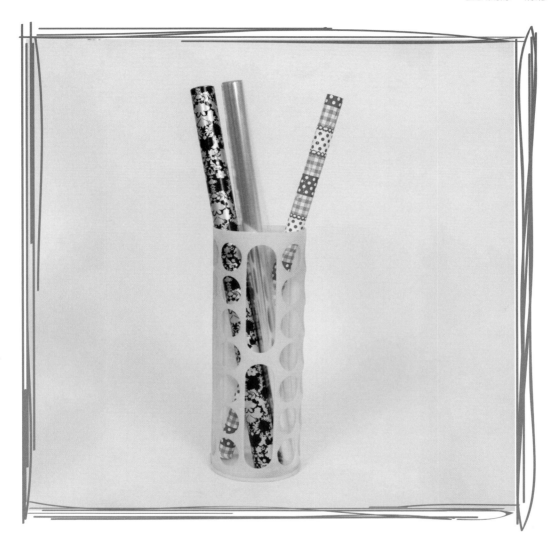

A BAG HOLDER BECOMES A STORAGE BIN FOR GIFT WRAP.

WHO NEEDS A COOKBOOK STAND WHEN YOU HAVE A PANTS HANGER?

SORRY, ALL YOU MAKERS OF LONG MATCHES, BUT A PIECE OF
DRY SPAGHETTI DOES THE JOB JUST FINE.

A PLAIN OLD PALLET BECOMES A SHOE RACK!

CAN'T TELL WHICH SIDE OF THE WINDOW THOSE ANNOYING STREAKS ARE ON? NEXT TIME YOU CLEAN, WIPE THE INSIDE FROM LEFT TO RIGHT, AND THE OUTSIDE FROM TOP TO BOTTOM. YOU'LL NEVER HAVE TO GUESS AGAIN!

A SIMPLE SPOON
BECOMES A DOORSTOP.

IS YOUR CAT USING THE PLANTS AS A RESTROOM?
HE WHO WON'T HEAR SHALL FEEL.

AN EMPTY PLASTIC BOTTLE OR GLASS JAR CAN BE
A MINI GREENHOUSE—FOR FREE!

PLUCKING ROSE PETALS ONE AT A TIME?
THERE'S AN EASIER WAY: GRAB THE ROSE
WITH ONE HAND, TAKE THE STEM WITH
THE OTHER HAND, TWIST, AND SHOW
YOUR ROMANTIC SOUL TO THE WORLD.

TO KEEP YOUR ARTFULLY ARRANGED BLOSSOMS IN PLACE, MAKE A
LATTICE PATTERN OUT OF CLEAR TAPE OVER THE VASE'S MOUTH.

EMPTY BOTTLE + A FEW
POKED HOLES + GARDEN HOSE
=
OUTDOOR SPRINKLER!

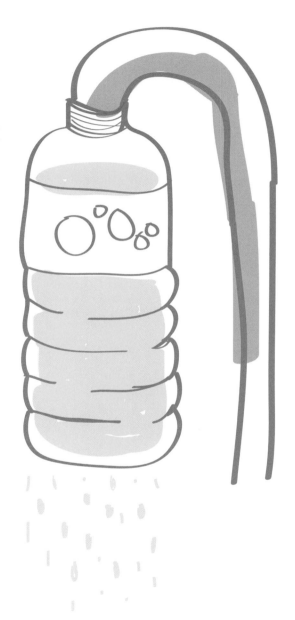

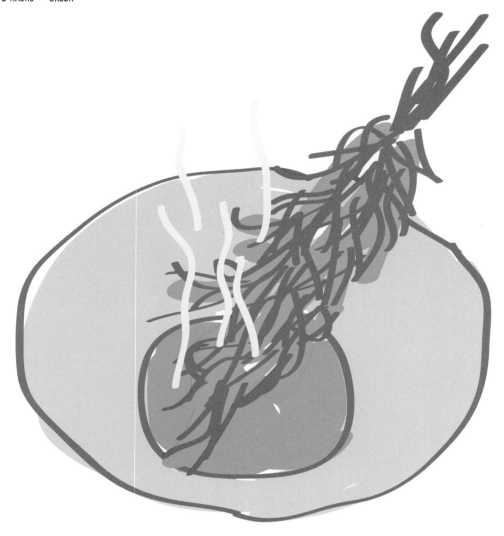

WANT TO KEEP CRITTERS FROM FLYING AROUND YOUR CAMPFIRE?
GATHER A BUNCH OF DRIED SAGE AND PUT IT IN THE FIRE.
THE SAGE SMOKE WILL KEEP UNWANTED VISITORS AWAY!

ADD A FEW DROPS OF VODKA OR BLEACH AND A TEASPOON OF SUGAR TO
THE WATER AND YOUR FLOWERS WILL STAY FRESH LONGER. PRETTY NEAT, NO?

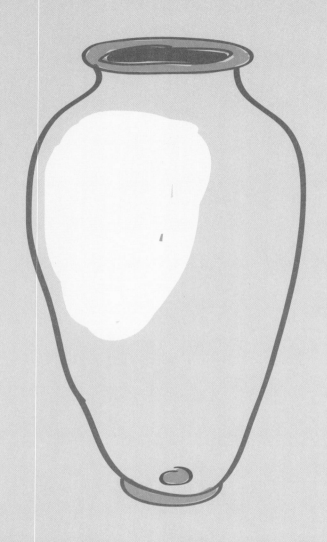

THE PREVIOUS TRICK ALSO ELIMINATES A BAD SMELL IN THE VASE.
AND WHILE THE BOTTLE IS OUT, VODKA MARTINIS ANYONE?

STEP 1: TIE A FEW PIECES OF WOOL YARN TOGETHER.
STEP 2: HANG THEM IN A BUCKET FILLED WITH WATER
         AND LET THE ENDS FALL INTO YOUR PLANTS.
STEP 3: TAKE A VACATION!

COOLED COOKING WATER FROM VEGETABLES, EGGS, OR POTATOES = NUTRITIOUS FOOD AND DRINK FOR YOUR PLANTS.

UPGRADE A PALLET INTO A GARDEN TOOL RACK!

SNAILS DON'T LIKE A FENCE MADE OF GROUND EGGSHELLS.
AND I DON'T LIKE SNAILS IN MY PLANTS. WIN-WIN!

THINK TWO BOWLS WON'T FIT IN THE MICROWAVE? THINK AGAIN!

SUMMERTIME IS FRUIT FLIES TIME! UNTIL NOW. MIX A LITTLE HONEY, BEER, AND A PIECE OF RIPE FRUIT (BANANA WORKS WELL) IN A SMALL BOWL. COVER WITH A PIECE OF PLASTIC WRAP AND PRICK A FEW HOLES IN IT. FRUIT FLIES CAN GO IN BUT THEY CAN'T GET OUT!

BECAUSE THAT LAST LITTLE SPRIG OF THYME IS ALWAYS IMPOSSIBLE TO FIND.
STORE IT IN A TEA STRAINER SPOON SO IT DOESN'T GO MISSING!

WANT WHIPPED CREAM BUT NO WHISK HANDY?
CREAM + JAR + SHAKE FOR 3 MINUTES. READY!

TURN TAB. STRAW IN. STRAW STAYS IN PLACE. TA-DA!

YOU CAN CUT TORTILLAS OR PITA BREAD INTO WEDGES.
THEY'LL BE EASY TO EAT, LIKE PIZZA!

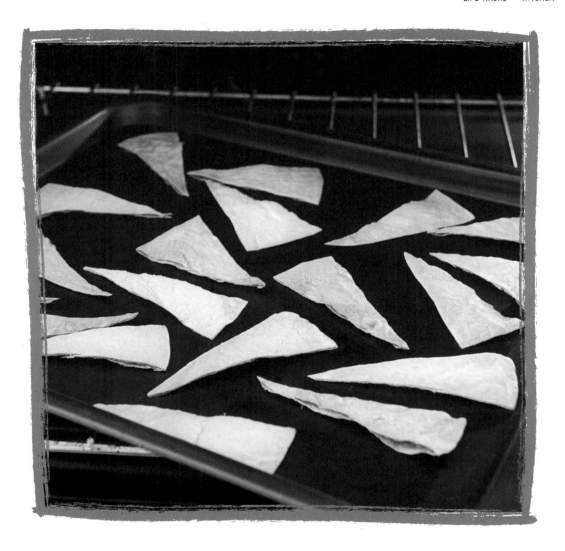

AND WHILE YOU'RE WORKING WITH TORTILLA WEDGES, YOU CAN BAKE THEM UNTIL CRISPY—KIND OF LIKE CHIPS, JUST A LITTLE HEALTHIER!

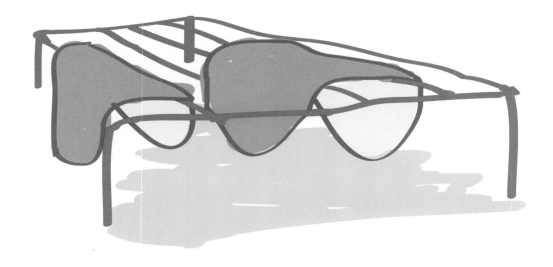

PLACE TORTILLAS ON AN OVEN RACK AND VOILÀ!
TORTILLAS TRANSFORMED INTO CRISPY TACO SHELLS.

LARGE LEMONADE PITCHERS CALL FOR LARGE ICE CUBES! FILL A MUFFIN PAN
WITH WATER AND LEMON WEDGES AND/OR FRAGRANT HERBS. PLACE IT IN
THE FREEZER AND POP OUT THE CUBES WHEN THEY'RE FROZEN. REFRESHING!

AND HERE YOU HAVE IT. THIS IS WHY THERE IS A NOTCH IN THE LID.

EVEN BETTER: WHEN YOU ARE DONE EATING THE CANDY,
YOU HAVE A GREAT TRAVEL-SIZE HERB CONTAINER.

SPAGHETTI + EMPTY CYLINDRICAL CHIPS BOX = A MATCH MADE IN HEAVEN.

BOILING WATER IN AN ELECTRIC KETTLE INSTEAD OF ON THE STOVETOP USES 30 PERCENT LESS ENERGY. IT'S ALSO MUCH FASTER.

CUT PINEAPPLE SLICES
BEFORE EMPTYING THE
CAN. MUCH EASIER!

A WAY TO PREVENT APPLES FROM TURNING AN ICKY BROWN COLOR WHEN YOU SLICE THEM? YES, IT EXISTS, AND ITS NAME IS "RUBBER BAND."

STALE CHIPS + OVEN = CRISPY CHIPS. BECAUSE HEY, THERE'S NEVER A GOOD REASON TO THROW AWAY CHIPS.

SUGAR WON'T BECOME HARD IF YOU FILL A BAG (AN EMPTY TEA BAG, FOR INSTANCE) WITH UNCOOKED RICE GRAINS AND ADD IT TO THE JAR.

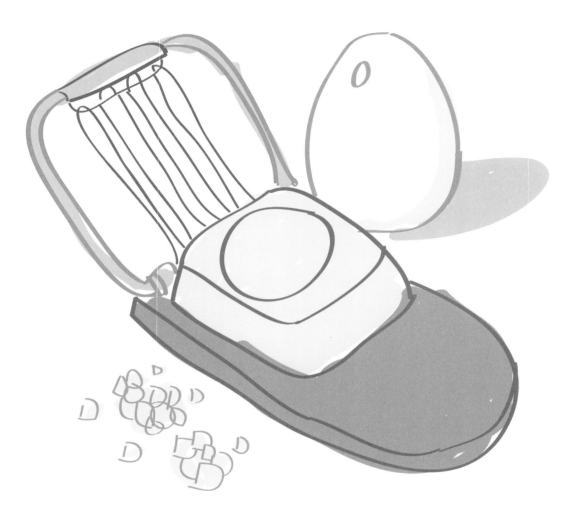

THINKING OUTSIDE THE BOX — PART 1: SLICE YOUR EGGS BOTH HORIZONTALLY AND VERTICALLY IN YOUR EGG SLIDER. HELLO EGG SALAD!

THINKING OUTSIDE THE BOX — PART 2: AN EGG SLICER ALSO SLICES KIWI. AND MUSHROOMS. AND BANANAS. AND STRAWBERRIES.

TURNS OUT THE BOTTOM OF YOUR MUFFIN PAN IS JUST AS GOOD AT MAKING TASTY TREATS AS THE TOP. MUFFIN PAN UPSIDE DOWN + COOKIE DOUGH CRUST DRAPED OVER IT = A SMALL BASKET FOR A SCOOP OF ICE CREAM!

WORRIED YOUR SODA CAN COULD EXPLODE? BEFORE OPENING,
TAP THE SIDE OF THE CAN A FEW TIMES WHILE TURNING IT.

NO MORE SCRUBBING THAT GRIMY MICROWAVE! SQUEEZE HALF
A LEMON INTO A MICROWAVE-SAFE BOWL OF WATER AND ADD
THE SLICES. HEAT ON HIGH FOR 5 MINUTES, THEN WIPE DOWN
YOUR MICROWAVE'S INTERIOR WITH A TOWEL. INSTANTLY CLEAN!

IF THE AREA AROUND THE STEM OF YOUR AVOCADO IS YELLOW-GREEN,
IT'S RIPE. IF IT IS DARK BROWN, MR. AVOCADO IS PAST HIS PRIME.

PIERCE A STRAWBERRY WITH A STRAW TO REMOVE
THE STEM, AIMING FROM BOTTOM TO TOP.
NOW THAT'S WHAT I CALL A "STRAW"-BERRY!

TYPICAL. YOU ARE AT THE CAMPGROUND WITH A NICE BOTTLE OF WINE, AND YOU FORGOT THE CORKSCREW! NO WORRIES: FINALLY, A GOOD REASON TO PULL OUT YOUR POCKETKNIFE. PUSH THE BLADE AS DEEP AS POSSIBLE INTO THE CORK, TURN UPWARD, AND CHEERS!

SERVING DISH + WINE GLASS = CHIPS 'N' DIP!

HOMEMADE COOKIES GOING STALE? OH HECK NO! WRAP A SLICE OF BREAD IN A PAPER TOWEL AND SLIDE IT IN YOUR COOKIE TIN—IT WILL KEEP YOUR TREATS CRISPY FOR A LONGER TIME. CRISIS AVERTED.

NO IDEA HOW MUCH PASTA TO SERVE PER PERSON?
USE THE NECK OF A BEER BOTTLE AS A GAUGE!

WHO NEEDS SPECIALTY COOKIE CUTTERS WHEN YOU
HAVE GLASSES? JUST USE A CLEAN ONE, OF COURSE.

IF YOU NEED TO BLOW OFF SOME
STEAM, MAY WE SUGGEST CRUMBLING
SOME COOKIES? PLACE THEM IN
A CLEAN PLASTIC BAG, GRAB A
SAUCEPAN, AND GO FOR IT! YOU CAN
USE YOUR CRUMBS IN A PIE CRUST
OR AS AN ICE-CREAM TOPPING.

IS YOUR KNIFE DULL? SHARPEN IT AGAINST THE BASE
OF A CERAMIC COFFEE MUG OR AGAINST A PATIO TILE.

CORK IN THE BOTTLE = COFFEE FILTER IN YOUR GLASS.

IF YOU LEAVE A WOODEN SPOON ACROSS A POT WITH
BOILING WATER, YOUR POT WILL NOT OVERFLOW.

PEEL A MANGO LIKE A CHEF: SLICE OFF THE SIDES AND DISCARD THE PIT IN THE CENTER. CARVE BOTH SIDES INTO A CHECKERBOARD PATTERN, THEN TURN THEM INSIDE OUT SO THE CUBES PROTRUDE. SLICE OFF THE CUBES WITH A KNIFE OR A SPOON.

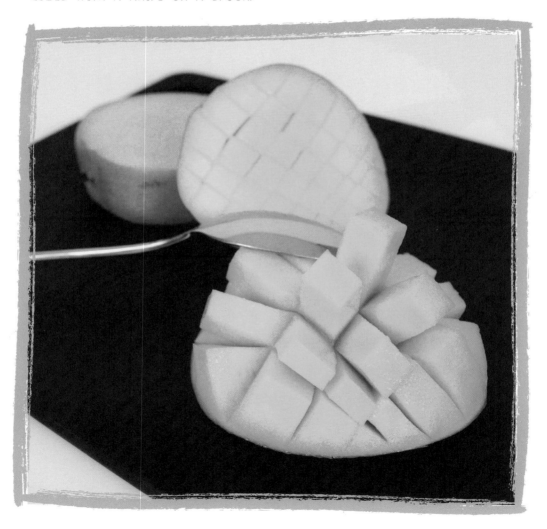

PEEL A MANGO LIKE A SUPER CHEF: TAKE ONE HALF OF THE MANGO AND HOLD IT WITH THE SKIN AS CLOSE AS POSSIBLE TO THE RIM OF THE GLASS. SLIDE THE MANGO FROM BOTTOM TO TOP ALONG THE GLASS AND TA-DA!

CAUTION: PEELING MANDARIN ORANGES WILL NEVER BE THE SAME AFTER YOU READ THIS. SLICE OFF THE TOP AND BOTTOM OF THE ORANGE, THEN MAKE AN INCISION FROM TOP TO BOTTOM, OPEN THE SKIN, AND UNFOLD A PERFECT ROW OF MANDARIN WEDGES!

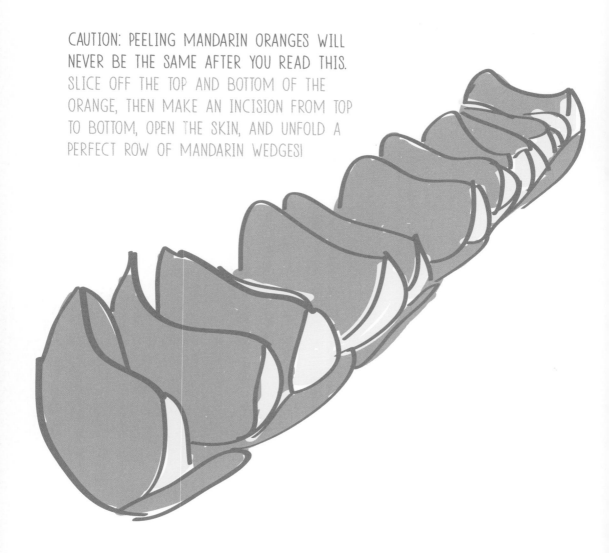

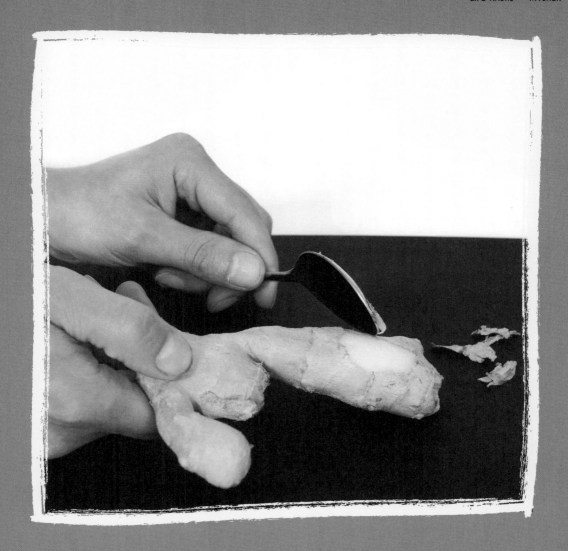

ACCESS THOSE HARD-TO-REACH SPOTS ON FRESH GINGER BY SCRAPING
OFF THE SKIN (AND ONLY THE SKIN) WITH A SPOON—RATHER THAN WASTING
THE DELICIOUS ROOT WITH A KNIFE OR PEELER. TOP PERFORMANCE!

RESCUE YOUR HERBS! FREEZE THEM! ADD A LITTLE OLIVE OIL AND YOU WILL ALWAYS HAVE HERB CUBES ON HAND. NOTE: ALSO WORKS WELL WITH TOMATO PASTE.

YOU CAN ALSO FREEZE YOUR HERBS WHOLE IN A PLASTIC BAG. BREAK THEM APART AS NEEDED, USING YOUR HANDS, A ROLLING PIN, OR A GLASS BOTTLE. READY FOR THE PAN!

HALF MARSHMALLOWS ON YOUR MUFFINS = TOPPING FOR LAZY COOKS!

IS THE NUTCASE IN YOU
WORRIED ABOUT COOKIES OF
DIFFERENT SHAPES? A MUFFIN
PAN IS WHAT YOU NEED.

AND IF YOU HAVE LEFTOVER COOKIE DOUGH,
JUST FREEZE IT IN BAKE-READY PORTIONS!

CUT YOUR CAKE OR PIE WITH DENTAL FLOSS.
(JUST NOT THE MINT-FLAVORED KIND, OF COURSE!)

IN THE "GREAT FRIED EGGS FOR BEGINNER COOKS" CATEGORY, FRY YOUR EGG INSIDE A SLICE OF BELL PEPPER.

IN THE "GREAT FRIED EGGS FOR ADVANCED COOKS" CATEGORY,
FRY YOUR EGG INSIDE A COOKIE CUTTER.

STEP 1: STICK A BOTTLE OF SUGARY, CONGEALED HONEY UPSIDE DOWN
IN A GLASS OF WARM WATER.
STEP 2: LET IT SIT FOR A FEW MINUTES.
STEP 3: GIVE IT A GOOD SQUEEZE AND WATCH THE HONEY FLOW.

PUT PLASTIC WRAP AROUND THE TOP OF A BANANA BUNCH—IT WILL KEEP THEM FRESH FOR AN EXTRA 5 DAYS. NO KIDDING.

CLEANING YOUR GRILL GRATES? WAIT UNTIL THE GRILL HAS COOLED BUT IS STILL SOMEWHAT WARM, THEN RUB IT DOWN WITH A BALL OF ALUMINUM FOIL DIPPED IN LEMON JUICE.

AND AFTER GRILLING, IF YOU'RE TOO LAZY (OR HAD TOO MUCH TO DRINK) TO CLEAN UP, SIMPLY PLACE YOUR GRATES ON THE GRASS. DEW WILL DO (PART OF) THE JOB FOR YOU!

SEPARATE YOUR BANANAS: THEY
WILL STAY FRESH LONGER THAN
A WHOLE BUNCH.

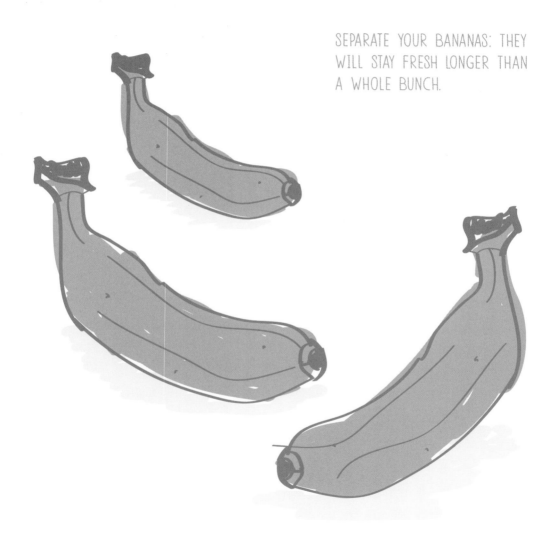

DO YOU USUALLY OPEN YOUR BANANAS FROM THE STEM—AND END UP WITH BRUISED FRUIT? TRY OPENING IT FROM THE BOTTOM...JUST LIKE MONKEYS DO!

SEPARATING EGGS, CHAMPION LEVEL: BREAK THE EGG INTO A SMALL BOWL. TAKE AN EMPTY WATER BOTTLE, HOLD THE OPENING OVER THE EGG YOLK, AND GIVE THE BOTTLE A GOOD SQUEEZE AND SUCK UP THE YOLK.

SPAGHETTI SAUCE IS DELICIOUS, BUT THE RED, MOLDY RESIDUE IT LEAVES IN YOUR PLASTIC CONTAINERS IS STRAIGHT-UP GROSS. MIX A DASH OF BLEACH WITH WATER, FILL THE CONTAINER WITH IT, AND PLACE IT IN THE FREEZER FOR A FEW DAYS. THE ICE WILL TURN RED AND YOU CAN SCRAPE IT OUT!

THIS IS HOW YOU SLICE BELL PEPPERS:
STEP 1: CUT OFF THE BOTTOM AND SET YOUR PEPPER ON THE COUNTER.
STEP 2: SLICE OFF THE FOUR SIDES OF THE PEPPER.
        THE STEM AND SEEDS WILL COME LOOSE!

BUGS THREATENING YOUR LEMONADE? TURN OVER A PAPER MUFFIN CUP, PUT IT ON THE GLASS, AND PRICK A STRAW THROUGH THE MIDDLE.

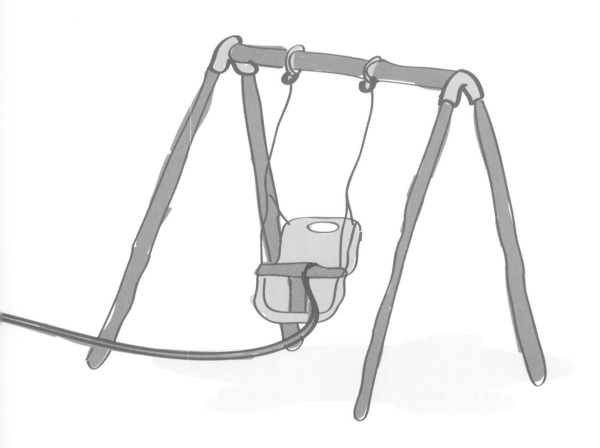

IF BABY'S HAPPY, MAMA'S HAPPY! TIE A ROPE TO THE SWING
SO YOU CAN SWING BABY FROM YOUR PATIO.

DOES YOUR KID ROLL OUT OF BED ALL THE TIME?
PLACE A SWIM NOODLE UNDER THE FITTED SHEET.

POPSICLES ARE THE BEST, STICKY HANDS ARE THE WORST.
USE MUFFIN CUPS TO CATCH THOSE DRIPS!

RECIPE FOR A CHILD-SIZE HOMEMADE HAMMOCK: TIE A PIECE OF FABRIC TO SOME ROPE, HANG THE ROPE AROUND A TABLE, AND VOILÀ!

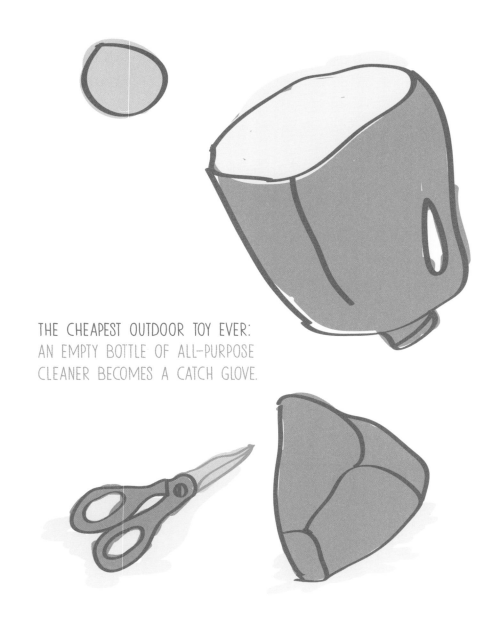

THE CHEAPEST OUTDOOR TOY EVER:
AN EMPTY BOTTLE OF ALL-PURPOSE
CLEANER BECOMES A CATCH GLOVE.

ONESIES HAVE ENVELOPE FOLDS AT THE NECK SO THAT YOU CAN ROLL
THE ONESIE **DOWNWARD** WHEN YOUR BABY MAKES A MESS THAT
EXCEEDS DIAPER CAPACITY—NOT **UPWARD** OVER BABY'S HEAD!

PAINT IN EGG CARTONS = NO CLEAN UP AFTERWARDS!

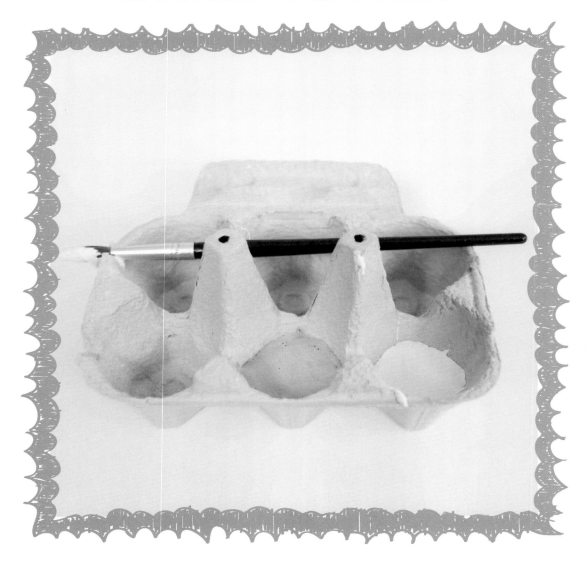

FACT #1: LITTLE GIRLS LOVE GLITTER.
FACT #2: MAMAS HATE GLITTER.
FACT #3: ALL MAMAS OF LITTLE GIRLS NEED A LINT ROLLER. NOW!

CONDITIONER SOFTENS KIDS' HAIR, SO WHY NOT YOUR KIDS' DOLLS' HAIR?
NOTE: WORKS WELL ON PAINTBRUSHES TOO.

POPSICLES IN SMALL YOGURT CONTAINERS = TOUCHDOWN!

DON'T LIKE GRIMY BATHTUB TOYS? GLUE THE LITTLE HOLE AT THE BOTTOM SHUT (WITH A GLUE GUN) BEFORE USING THEM.

DRIED MARKERS WILL GET A SECOND LIFE AS WATERCOLOR BRUSHES
IF YOU SOAK THEM IN A CUP OF WATER FOR 24 HOURS.

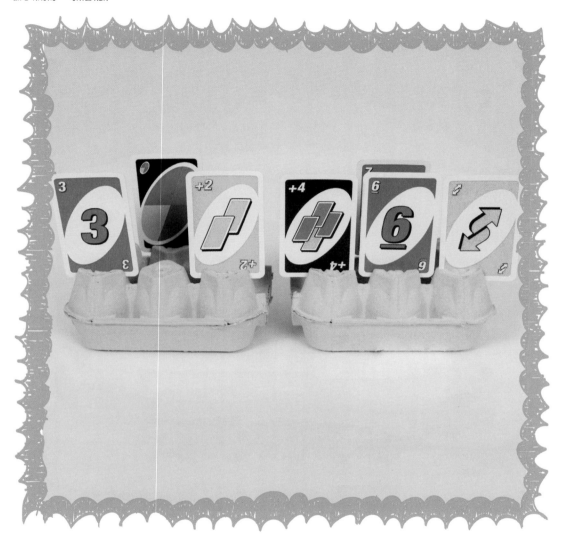

SMALL CHILDREN'S HANDS STRUGGLING TO HOLD A HAND OF CARDS?
EGGS TO THE RESCUE! TURN AN EGG CARTON UPSIDE DOWN AND USE
A BOX CUTTER TO MAKE A LONG SLIT BETWEEN THE LITTLE MOUNDS,
THEN SLIDE THE CARDS IN.

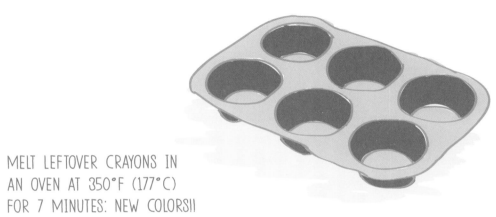

MELT LEFTOVER CRAYONS IN
AN OVEN AT 350°F (177°C)
FOR 7 MINUTES: NEW COLORS!!

SUNSCREEN SPRAY BOTTLE EMPTY?
USE IT AS A WATER SPRAY.

LITTLE SHOES ALWAYS ON THE WRONG FOOT? NO MORE!
CUT A LARGE STICKER IN HALF AND PUT ONE PART IN
EACH SHOE. DRAW A HALF HEART IN EACH.

GOT A PLASTIC BAG? YOU'VE GOT A SMOCK FOR MESSES!

MAKE YOUR OWN KINETIC SAND—THAT WACKY, WONDERFUL,
ENDLESSLY MOLDABLE STUFF KIDS LOVE. SIMPLY MIX
ALL-PURPOSE FLOUR WITH A LITTLE BABY OIL AND KNEAD.

CLOGGED SHOWERHEAD? ATTACH A PLASTIC BAG FILLED WITH VINEGAR
AND WATER TO THE SHOWERHEAD AND LET SIT FOR A FEW HOURS.

DOES YOUR RING LEAVE GREEN SPOTS ON YOUR FINGERS?
APPLY A LAYER OF CLEAR NAIL POLISH TO THE INSIDE OF THE RING.

MORE SMART HACKS WITH CLEAR NAIL POLISH: SMEAR IT ON
THE HOOKS OR POSTS OF YOUR EARRINGS, AND EVEN THE MOST
SENSITIVE EARLOBES WILL TOLERATE ANY EARRING.

DID YOU JUST BUY A NEW SHIRT? APPLY A LITTLE CLEAR NAIL POLISH ON THE BUTTONS AND YOU'LL NEVER LOSE THEM!

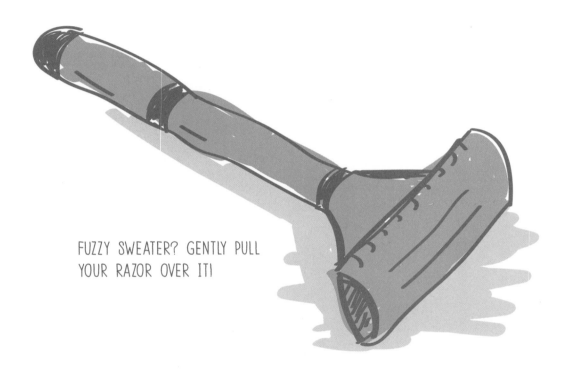

FUZZY SWEATER? GENTLY PULL YOUR RAZOR OVER IT!

PLACE DRIED TEA BAGS IN YOUR SHOES = BYE BYE STINKY SNEAKERS!

TO REMOVE LIME SPOTS ON YOUR FIXTURES, RUB A HALF LEMON OVER THEM (AND USE THE OTHER HALF FOR A NICE CUP OF LEMON TEA TO REWARD YOURSELF FOR ALL THE SO-CALLED SCRUBBING).

FOR PAINLESS PLUCKING, RUB AN ICE CUBE OVER YOUR EYEBROWS BEFORE HAVING AT THEM WITH TWEEZERS.

TO COVER UP A NASTY SMELL IN THE BATHROOM, LIGHT A MATCH!

EASY TRICK TO CLEAN OUT YOUR CLOSET: THE NEXT TIME YOU REORGANIZE
YOUR CLOTHES, MAKE SURE ALL YOUR HANGERS HAVE THEIR HOOKS TURNED
THE SAME WAY. EVERY TIME YOU WEAR AN ITEM, HANG IT BACK WITH
THE HOOK REVERSED. EVERY GARMENT WHOSE HANGER IS IN THE INITIAL
POSITION AFTER ONE YEAR MUST GO!

DOUBLE TAKE: EMPTY WATER BOTTLES MAKE GREAT BOOT STRETCHERS!

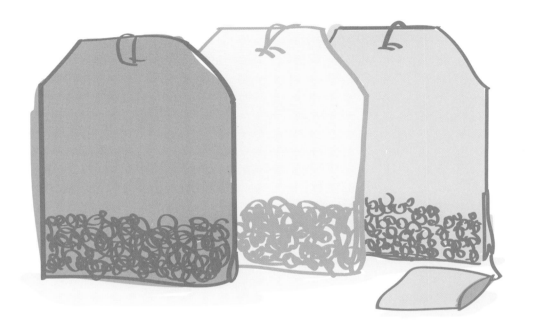

TEA BAG BECOMES EYE MASK
STEP 1: DRINK A CUP OF BLACK OR HERBAL TEA.
STEP 2: LET THE USED TEA BAGS COOL IN THE REFRIGERATOR.
STEP 3: PLACE THEM OVER YOUR EYES FOR 5 MINUTES.
STEP 4: GOODBYE PUFFY EYES!

BUILT-UP LINT IN YOUR BLOW-DRYER? NO
IDEA HOW TO CLEAN THE LITTLE GRID?
THREE WORDS: YOUR OLD TOOTHBRUSH.

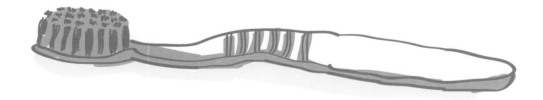

AN OLD TRICK FROM THEATER PEOPLE: TO MASK A SWEATY ODOR,
POUR A LITTLE VODKA IN A SPRAY BOTTLE, SPRAY IT ON THE GARMENT,
AND YOU'RE GOOD TO GO—AT LEAST UNTIL THE NEXT LAUNDRY BATCH.

TIGHT PUMPS + A THICK PAIR OF SOCKS + BLOW–DRYER
+ 10 MINUTES OF YOUR TIME = BETTER–FITTING PUMPS!

SUGAR OR SALT +
VEGETABLE OIL +
ESSENTIAL OIL =
THE BEST SCRUB EVER!

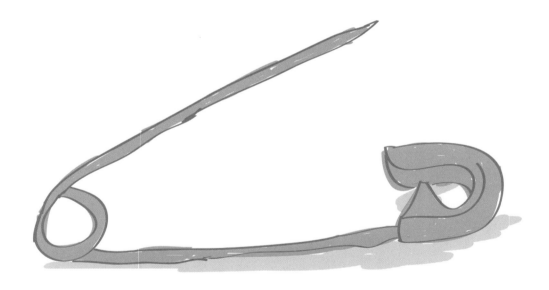

THE STORY OF THE HOODIE AND THE LOST DRAWSTRING:
ATTACH A SAFETY PIN AT ONE END OF THE DRAWSTRING.
SLIDE IT INTO THE CHANNEL AND PUSH IT ALL THE WAY TO THE END.

IS YOUR TOOTHPASTE TUBE ALMOST EMPTY? SLIDE A BOBBY PIN OVER
THE TUBE AND USE IT TO PUSH ANY LEFTOVER PASTE UP TO THE OPENING.

BY THE WAY, IF THE TIC-TAC BOX FROM PAGE 48 IS EMPTY,
YOU HAVE A GREAT LITTLE CONTAINER FOR YOUR BOBBY PINS.

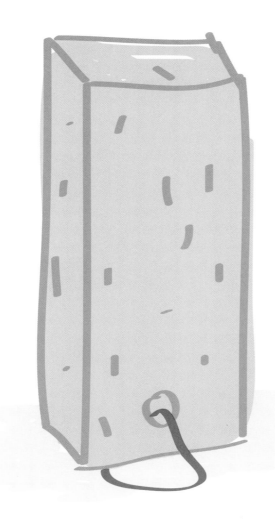

MAYBE YOU SAW THE WHITE STICK ON YOUR DAD'S SHAVING TABLE: THE
ALUM BLOCK. ALUM IS A NATURAL STONE USED TO HEAL SMALL CUTS FROM
SHAVING. BUT DID YOU KNOW THAT ALUM ALSO WORKS GREAT AS FRAGRANT-
FREE DEODORANT? LIGHTLY WET THE STICK AND APPLY IT ON YOUR ARMPITS.

WRINKLED T-SHIRT AND NO IRON ON HAND? PLACE IT ON A HANGER IN THE BATHROOM AND TAKE A HOT SHOWER. THE STEAM WILL ERASE ALL WRINKLES!

SO YOU FINALLY BOUGHT THESE NICE NEW BALLERINA FLATS. NOW YOU'RE READY TO GO DANCING, BUT YOU NOTICE THAT THE SUCKERS HAVE DANGEROUSLY SLICK SOLES! A PIECE OF STRONG, WIDE TAPE TO THE RESCUE.

DO YOU HAVE AN URGENT
LAUNDRY BATCH? AND
YOU ARE OUT OF FABRIC
SOFTENER? NO PROBLEM.
HALF A CUP (120 ML)
OF VINEGAR WORKS TOO!

IF YOU IMITATE A PERSON'S BODY LANGUAGE,
THAT PERSON WILL LISTEN TO YOU BETTER.

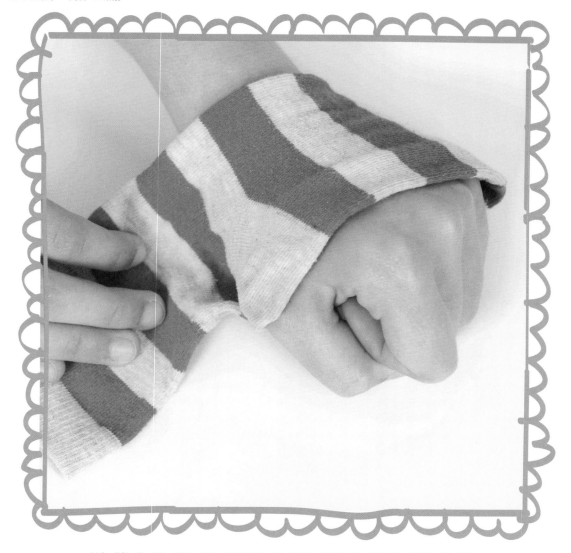

NO TIME TO TRY ON SOCKS IN THE STORE? WRAP THE SOCK AROUND YOUR LEFT FIST. IF YOU CAN EASILY CLOSE THE CIRCLE, THE SOCK WILL FIT YOUR FOOT.

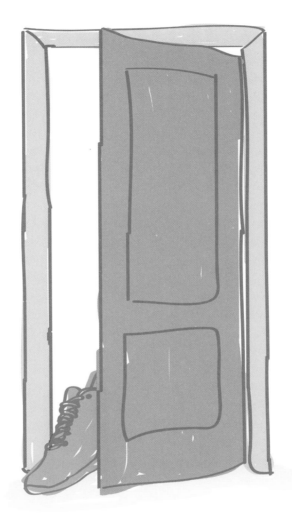

A GREAT TRICK IF YOU WANT TO ASK TWO THINGS FROM SOMEBODY: ASK THE EASIEST FIRST, THEN ASK THE HARDER THING. THIS IS CALLED THE FOOT-IN-THE-DOOR TECHNIQUE.

OTHER METHOD: FIRST, ASK SOMETHING IMPOSSIBLE. THEN ASK WHAT YOU REALLY WANT THAT PERSON TO DO FOR YOU. HE OR SHE WILL NOT AGREE TO THE IMPOSSIBLE TASK BUT WILL TAKE THE EASIER ONE.

SNEEZE NOT COMING OUT? LOOK TOWARD THE LIGHT!

PLAYING ROCK-PAPER-SCISSORS? HERE ARE A FEW TRICKS:
- IS IT A MAN WHO DOESN'T KNOW THE GAME WELL?
  HE WILL PROBABLY CHOOSE ROCK, SO YOU SHOULD CHOOSE PAPER.
- IS IT A WOMAN WHO DOESN'T KNOW THE GAME WELL?
  THERE IS GREAT CHANCE SHE WILL GO FOR THE SCISSORS. THEN YOU TAKE THE ROCK.
- A FORMIDABLE, EXPERIENCED ADVERSARY?
  YOUR CHANCES ARE HIGHER IF YOU BEGIN WITH SCISSORS.

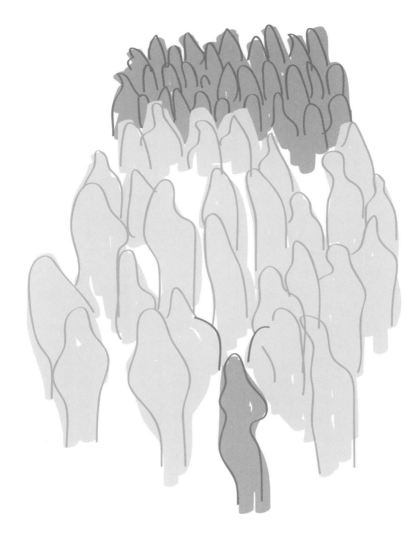

STUCK IN A CROWD? LOOK OVER THE SHOULDERS OF THE PEOPLE AROUND YOU, OR DIRECT YOUR GAZE BETWEEN THE HEADS OF TWO INDIVIDUALS. THIS WAY, YOU INDICATE THAT YOU ARE ON THE GO AND PEOPLE WILL LET YOU GO THROUGH FASTER.

WHEN YOU'RE HEADED TOWARD THE CHECKOUT, CHOOSE THE LEFT LINE. MOST PEOPLE, BEING RIGHT-HANDED, UNCONSCIOUSLY GET INTO THE RIGHT LINE.

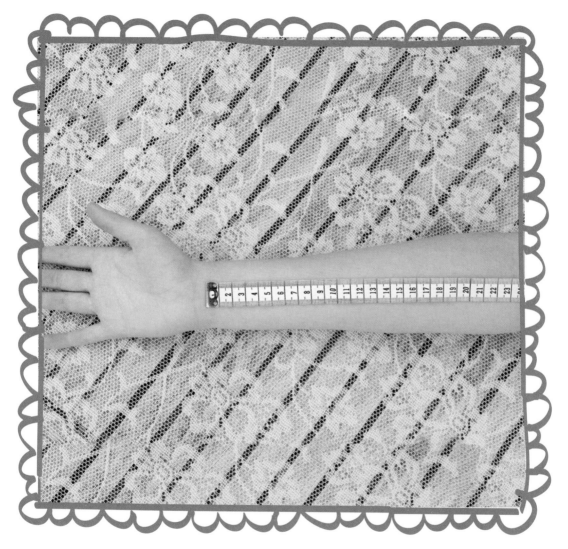

WANT TO KNOW HOW LONG YOUR FOOT IS WITHOUT REACHING
FOR YOUR FOOT? MEASURE THE LENGTH OF YOUR FOREARM
FROM YOUR ELBOW TO YOUR WRIST (I BET YOU ARE PUTTING
THIS BOOK ASIDE RIGHT NOW TO TRY THIS ;-)).

A HALF-ONION ON YOUR NIGHT STAND MAY HELP
YOU FIGHT OFF AN ONCOMING COLD.

ALL OF US CAN USE REVERSE PSYCHOLOGY EVERY ONCE IN A WHILE.
THIS DOESN'T WORK: TELLING YOUR DAUGHTER, "PUT YOUR SWEATER ON!"
THIS WORKS: "TODAY, WOULD YOU RATHER WEAR THE RED ONE OR THE WHITE ONE?"
RESULT: SHE PUTS A SWEATER ON. AND THAT IS EXACTLY WHAT YOU WANT!
THIS ALSO WORKS WITH COLLEAGUES AND EVEN—MAYBE—WITH YOUR BETTER HALF.

PICKING UP PIZZA? SWITCH ON YOUR SEAT WARMER!

DO YOU WANT TO LET YOUR JUST-WASHED WINTER COAT DRY IN THE SPRING SUN? PLACE TWO HANGERS TOGETHER WITH THE HOOKS FACING EACH OTHER, AND HANG YOUR JACKET ON THEM. EVEN THE STIFFEST SPRING BREEZE WON'T BLOW IT OFF THE HANGERS!

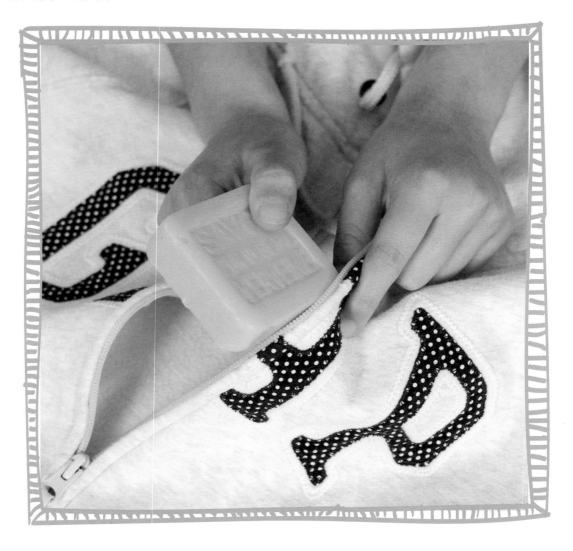

ZIPPER STUCK? RUB THE CRIME SCENE WITH A CANDLE, A BAR OF SOAP, OR A PENCIL, AND YOUR ZIPPER WILL SLIDE LIKE A CHARM.

THIS IS A TIP FROM MY MOTHER: IF YOU'RE OUT WALKING AT NIGHT, ALWAYS CARRY A SUGAR CUBE IN YOUR COAT POCKET. A SCRATCH MADE WITH A SUGAR CUBE WILL LEAVE A BLOODY SCAR ON A POTENTIAL ATTACKER'S CHEEK, WHICH WILL RESULT IN EITHER A) HIM RUNNING AWAY OR B) THE POLICE EASILY IDENTIFYING HIM.

THE BEACH IS GREAT. THE SAND ALL OVER YOUR BODY AFTERWARD...NOT SO MUCH. SO SPREAD SOME TALCUM POWDER ON YOUR BODY WHEN YOU LEAVE. THE SAND WILL FALL OFF!

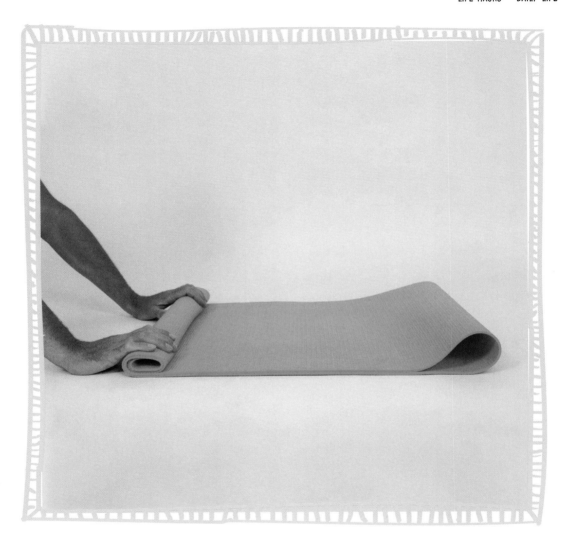

FOLD YOUR YOGA MAT IN HALF AND ROLL IT UP. NO MORE
IRRITATING CURLED-UP ENDS DURING YOUR NEXT DOWNWARD DOG!

ARE YOU THE ABSENT-MINDED TYPE WHO ALWAYS FORGETS TO RETURN BORROWED TOOLS? NEXT TIME, TAKE A PICTURE OF THE PERSON WITH THE LOANED ITEM.

ON A HOT SUMMER DAY, FASTEN YOUR SEAT BELT EVEN
IF YOU AREN'T IN THE CAR—UNLESS YOU WANT TO BE
BRANDED PERMANENTLY, OF COURSE.

IF YOU HAVE A SMALL DENT IN YOUR PING-PONG BALL, HOLD IT
UNDER RUNNING HOT WATER FOR A FEW SECONDS.

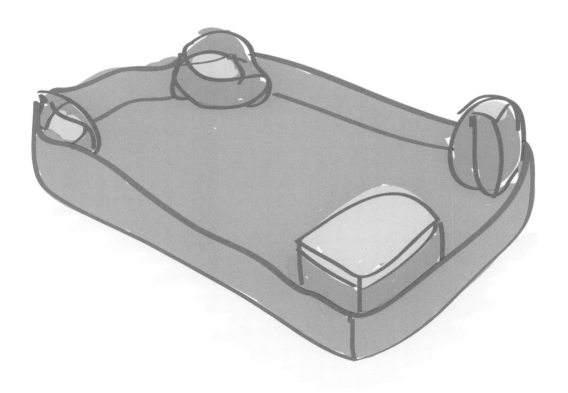

INSTEAD OF A BEACH TOWEL, TAKE A FITTED SHEET WITH
AN ELASTIC RIM. PLACE BAGS OR YOUR COOLER IN EACH
CORNER. SAND DOESN'T STAND A CHANCE!

DO YOU KEEP FORGETTING WHEN YOU LAST TOOK YOUR MEDICATION? THIS
SIMPLE BUT GENIUS TECHNIQUE IS INFALLIBLE! DRAW A SMALL GRID ON
THE BOX, WITH A BOX FOR EACH MOMENT WHEN YOU NEED TO TAKE
SOMETHING. THEN CHECK A BOX WHEN YOU SWALLOW THE PILL!

ALWAYS KEEP A STURDY LAUNDRY BASKET IN THE TRUNK OF YOUR CAR. YOU'LL AVOID MULTIPLE TRIPS BACK AND FORTH WHEN BRINGING YOUR GROCERIES INTO THE HOUSE.

YOUR BEER-BOTTLE TOWER WILL HOLD UP BETTER WITH A BINDER CLIP!
ATTACH IT TO THE FRIDGE SHELF NEXT TO THE FIRST BOTTOM BOTTLE.

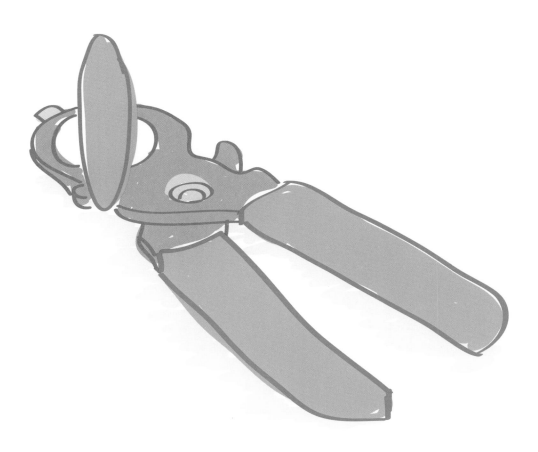

A HARD PLASTIC BLISTER PACK IS EASY TO OPEN WITH A CAN OPENER.

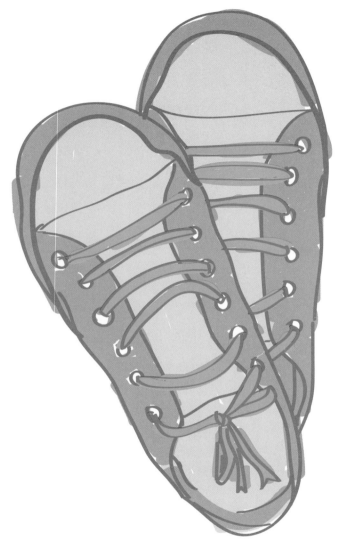

WHO EVER THOUGHT OF THIS?
NEXT TIME YOU TIE YOUR SHOE LACES, MAKE A LOOP AND WRAP THE
LACE AROUND THE OUTSIDE OF THE LOOP, NOT THE INSIDE LIKE YOU
WERE TAUGHT AS A KID. THE KNOT WILL BE FAR SUPERIOR!

DON'T STACK YOUR T-SHIRTS IN A PILE IN YOUR DRAWER. LINE THEM
UP VERTICALLY INSTEAD, SO YOU CAN VIEW THEM ALL INSTANTLY
AND WON'T JUST TAKE THE TOP T-SHIRT. BECAUSE T-SHIRTS AT THE
BOTTOM OF THE PILE ALSO DESERVE TO BE WORN!

STUBBORN LID ON YOUR JAR? TRY RUBBER GLOVES!

NEED A QUIET MOMENT TO WORK ON A PROJECT WITH A HARD DEADLINE? PUT HEADPHONES ON—THE BIGGER, THE BETTER. MUSIC OPTIONAL. (EITHER WAY, PEOPLE WILL NOT DISTURB YOU.)

ROTTEN CHORE IN YOUR NEAR FUTURE? THE POMODORO TECHNIQUE* SHALL SAVE YOU!
SET A TIMER FOR 25 MINUTES AND WORK AS HARD AS YOU CAN ON THE CHORE. GOOD,
YOU STARTED, PAT YOURSELF ON THE BACK! AFTER THIS FIRST "POMODORO," YOU DESERVE
A 3-MINUTE BREAK. THEN KEEP ON GOING. IF YOU COMPLETE 3 OR 4 POMODOROS,
YOU HAVE EARNED A 15-MINUTE BREAK!

*POMODORO REFERS TO THE TIMER OWNED BY THE INVENTOR OF THIS TECHNIQUE,
PROBABLY IN THE SHAPE OF A TOMATO. (THE TIMER, NOT THE INVENTOR! ;-P)

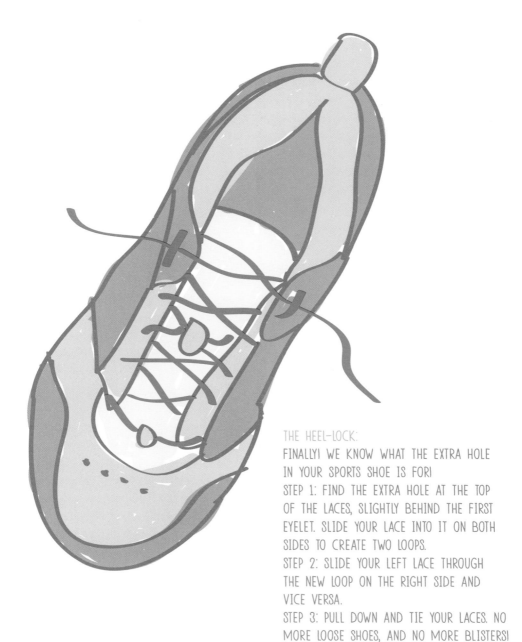

THE HEEL-LOCK:
FINALLY! WE KNOW WHAT THE EXTRA HOLE
IN YOUR SPORTS SHOE IS FOR!
STEP 1: FIND THE EXTRA HOLE AT THE TOP
OF THE LACES, SLIGHTLY BEHIND THE FIRST
EYELET. SLIDE YOUR LACE INTO IT ON BOTH
SIDES TO CREATE TWO LOOPS.
STEP 2: SLIDE YOUR LEFT LACE THROUGH
THE NEW LOOP ON THE RIGHT SIDE AND
VICE VERSA.
STEP 3: PULL DOWN AND TIE YOUR LACES. NO
MORE LOOSE SHOES, AND NO MORE BLISTERS!

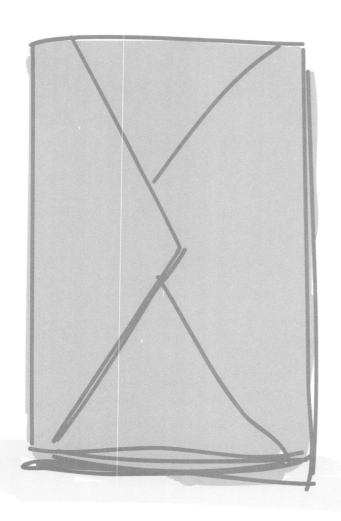

PUT AN ENVELOPE IN THE FREEZER FOR A FEW HOURS, AND YOU'LL BE ABLE TO OPEN IT WITHOUT TEARING IT!

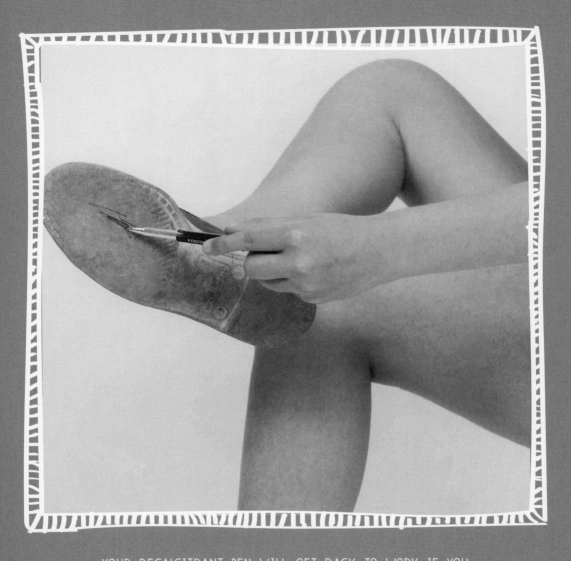

YOUR RECALCITRANT PEN WILL GET BACK TO WORK IF YOU
SCRIBBLE ON THE RUBBER SOLE OF YOUR SHOE.

A POTATO CHIP BAG IS NOT ONLY USEFUL FOR KEEPING THE CRISPY GOODNESS.
YOU CAN TURN IT INTO A SMALL BOWL BY FOLDING IN THE BOTTOM CORNERS
AND PUSHING THE BOTTOM UPWARD UNTIL THE CHIPS COME TO THE SURFACE.
READY TO SERVE!

IF YOU'RE TRYING TO HANG A FRAME
ON THE WALL WITH 2 HOOKS, YOU
MAY STRUGGLE TO FIND THE IDEAL
DISTANCE BETWEEN THEM.
STEP 1: PLACE A PIECE OF TAPE
BETWEEN THE HOLES ON THE
OUTER SIDE OF THE FRAME.
STEP 2: PUT A DOT WHERE EACH
OF THE HOLES ARE.
STEP 3: TAKE OFF THE TAPE AND
PUT IT ON THE WALL.
THERE YOU HAVE IT! YOU KNOW
EXACTLY WHERE TO DRILL.

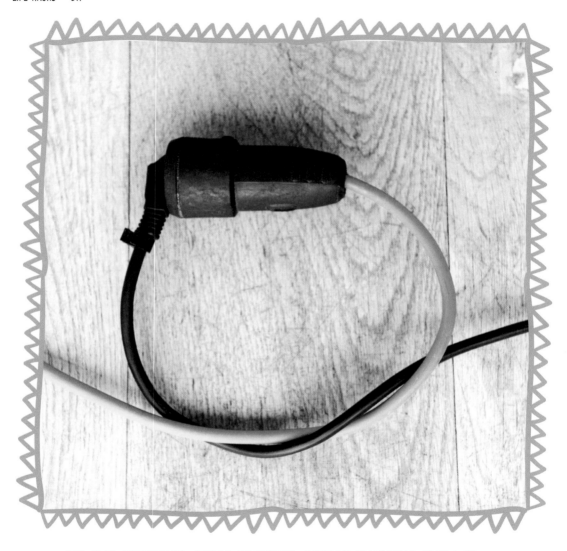

TIE TWO EXTENSION CORDS TOGETHER BEFORE PLUGGING THEM IN.
THEY'LL STAY CONNECTED EVEN IF YOU ACCIDENTALLY PULL ON
A CORD A LITTLE TOO HARD.

NOT SURE IF YOU'VE REMOVED ALL THE SPLINTERS FROM THE DOOR YOU'RE SANDING? RUB AN OLD PAIR OF NYLON PANTYHOSE OVER THE SURFACE. YOU'LL SEE THEM INSTANTLY.

CREATE A LUMINOUS PATH IN YOUR GARDEN BY PAINTING OR
SPRAYING A FEW STONES WITH GLOW-IN-THE-DARK PAINT.

DRILL HOLES WITHOUT DUST: HAVE A FRIEND HOLD YOUR VACUUM EXACTLY
UNDER THE HOLE AS YOU DRILL. IF YOU'RE ALONE, TAPE AN OPEN ENVELOPE
AGAINST THE WALL. INSTANT DUST-CATCHER!

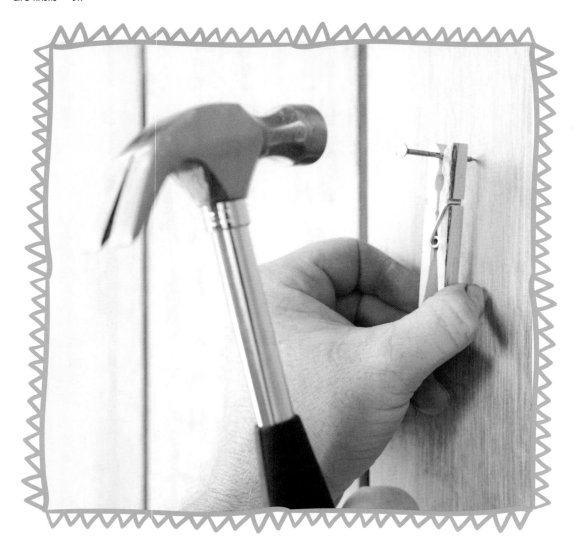

USE A CLOTHESPIN OR A COMB TO HOLD A NAIL
WHILE YOU HAMMER IT INTO THE WALL.

PAINT JOB? A TEASPOON OF VANILLA EXTRACT WILL MAKE
NO DIFFERENCE TO THE PAINT, BUT IT MAKES A HUGE
DIFFERENCE TO THE SMELL IN YOUR HOUSE!

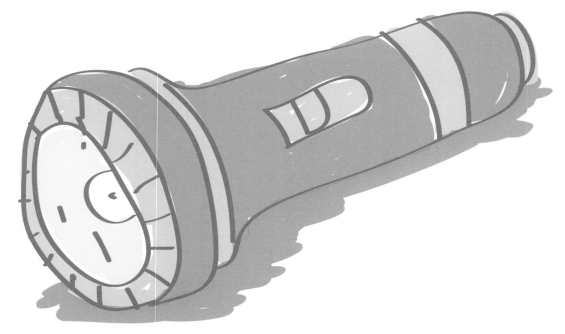

NEXT TIME YOU NEED TO CHECK THE
FUSES IN A DARK BASEMENT, TIE YOUR
FLASHLIGHT TO YOUR ARM WITH A WATCH
OR RUBBER BAND, MACGYVER-STYLE!

STRETCH A WIDE RUBBER BAND OVER THE PAINT CAN, SO YOU
CAN WIPE OFF YOUR BRUSH WITHOUT PAINTING THE POT!

INSTANT AMPLIFIERS FOR YOUR SMARTPHONE: A BOWL,
CUP, BUCKET, OR DRY WASHBASIN IN YOUR BATHROOM!

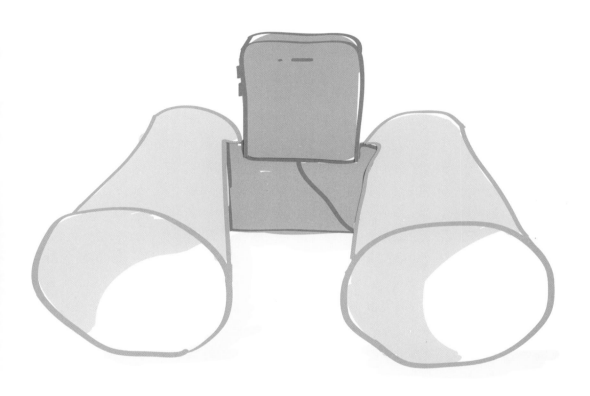

WANT TO IMPRESS YOUR FRIENDS? YOU NEED AN EMPTY TOILET PAPER ROLL AND TWO PLASTIC CUPS. CUT A SLIT THE LENGTH OF YOUR SMARTPHONE ALONG THE TOP OF THE ROLL. THEN CUT A HOLE THE SIZE OF THE TP ROLL IN EACH CUP, MAKING SURE IT FITS EXACTLY. STICK THE CUPS ON EITHER SIDE OF THE ROLL AND PLACE YOUR SMARTPHONE IN THE MIDDLE OF YOUR BEATBOX SYSTEM!

YOUR PHONE WILL CHARGE MUCH FASTER IF YOU SET IT ON AIRPLANE MODE!

DID THE FLAT SCREEN TV ENTER YOUR LIFE WITHOUT LEGS?
PLACE IT ON A GUITAR STAND.

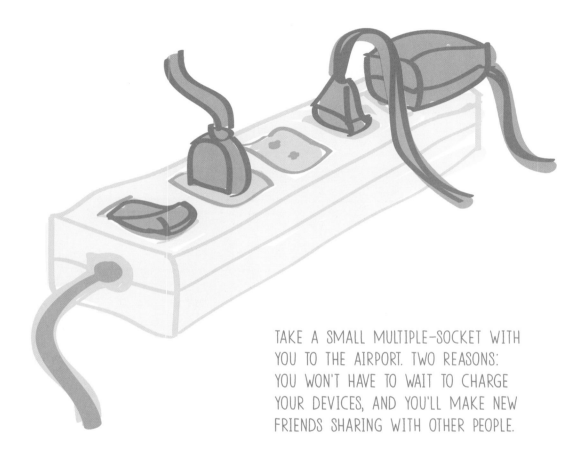

TAKE A SMALL MULTIPLE-SOCKET WITH
YOU TO THE AIRPORT. TWO REASONS:
YOU WON'T HAVE TO WAIT TO CHARGE
YOUR DEVICES, AND YOU'LL MAKE NEW
FRIENDS SHARING WITH OTHER PEOPLE.

YOU CAN FASTEN YOUR IPOD OR SMARTPHONE TO
THE FAN VENT IN YOUR CAR WITH A RUBBER BAND.

USE AN OLD CASSETTE CASE TO MAKE A HOLDER FOR YOUR SMARTPHONE. SIMPLY FOLD IT WITH ONE SIDE FLAT ON THE TABLE, AND THE OTHER AT AN ANGLE. THEN SLIDE YOUR PHONE IN!

ARE YOU TOO YOUNG FOR CASSETTE CASES? USE TWO LARGE
BINDER CLIPS. BOOM! A SMARTPHONE HOLDER!

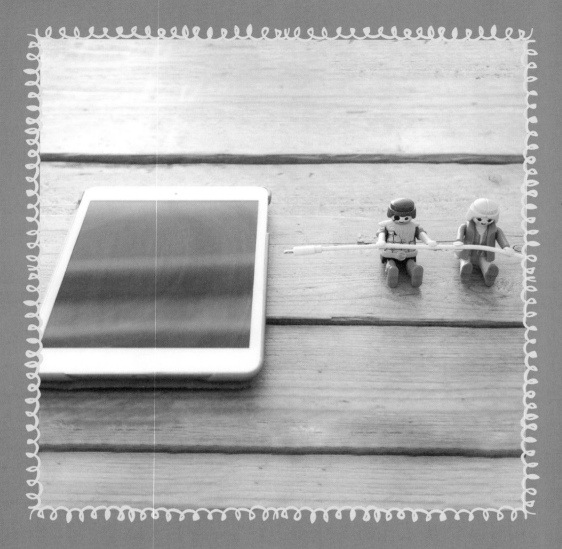

USE LITTLE LEGO, DUPLO, OR PLAYMOBIL PEOPLE TO HOLD THE
CORDS OF YOUR DEVICES. IF YOU USE THEM OFTEN, GLUE THEM
TO THE CABINET OR TABLE. ALSO CONVENIENT IN THE CAR.

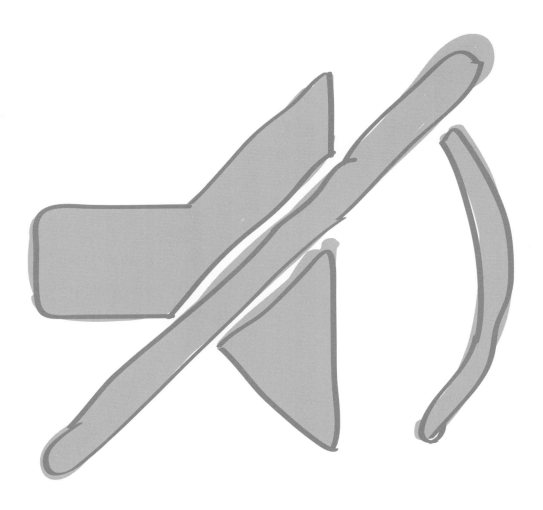

TURN OFF AS MANY BEEPS AND POP-UPS AS POSSIBLE. EVERY CALL OR NOTICE ROBS YOU OF 10 TO 20 MINUTES OF CONCENTRATION. THIS IS AT LEAST AS LONG AS IT TAKES FOR YOU TO GET BACK INTO FOCUS.

DO YOU ALWAYS TRAVEL WITH A POWDER COMPACT? INSERT A COTTON DISC IN THE CASE TO PROTECT IT FROM CRACKS AND BREAKS.

PUT YOUR JEWELRY IN A PILL BOX.

FREE DRINKS + A SMALLER ECOLOGICAL FOOTPRINT? YES, PLEASE.
TAKE AN EMPTY REFILLABLE WATER BOTTLE WITH YOU TO THE AIRPORT.
FILL IT WITH TAP WATER AFTER PASSING THROUGH THE SECURITY CHECK.

A ROLLED-UP BELT PLACED IN A FOLDED SHIRT IN YOUR SUITCASE =
A COLLAR WITHOUT CREASES!

ATTACH YOUR EARRINGS TO A LARGE BUTTON TO KEEP
THE FRONTS AND BACKS TEAMED UP TOGETHER.

ROLL YOUR CLOTHES INSTEAD OF FOLDING THEM
TO SAVE A TON OF ROOM IN YOUR SUITCASE!

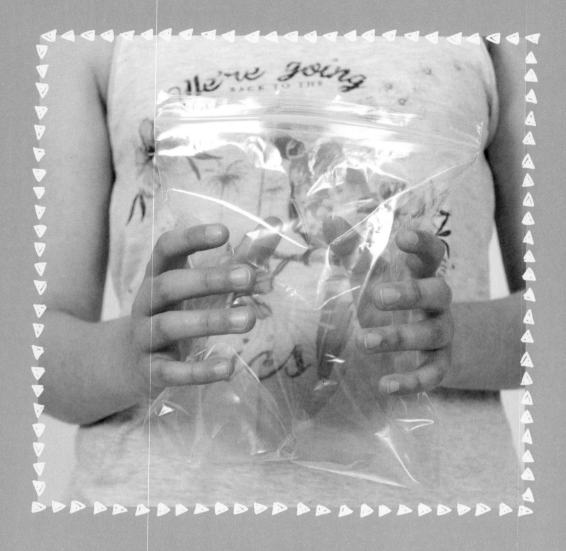

MOTION SICKNESS? YOUR TRAVELLING COMPANIONS WILL FIND
IT REALLY NICE IF YOU HAVE A ZIP-TOP BAG WITH YOU. YOU
KNOW, FOR KEEPING THE SMELL TO YOURSELF AND SUCH.

WWW.SEATGURU.COM LETS YOU CHOOSE THE BEST SEAT ON THE AIRPLANE.

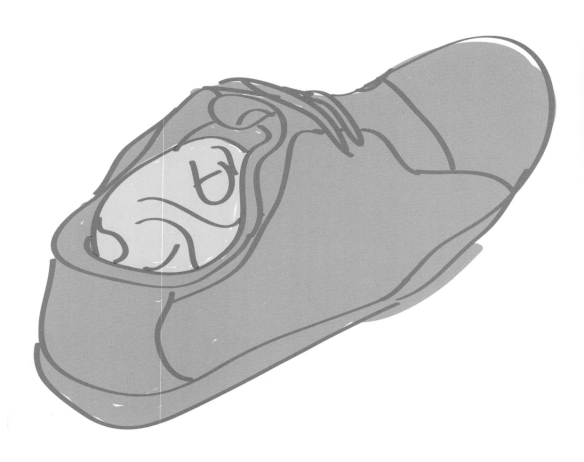

SOCKS IN YOUR SHOES = MORE SPACE IN THE SUITCASE + NO CRUSHED SHOES.

IF YOU ARE TRAVELING WITH YOUR WHOLE FAMILY, PACK THEIR STUFF
IN SEPARATE PLASTIC BAGS, EACH WITH THEIR OWN COLOR, BECAUSE
A) YOU DON'T END UP WITH A MESS IN YOUR SUITCASE (YOU ALWAYS
NEED THE ITEM THAT IS ALL THE WAY AT THE BOTTOM) AND
B) YOU INSTANTLY KNOW WHO HAS WHAT WHEN YOU UNPACK.

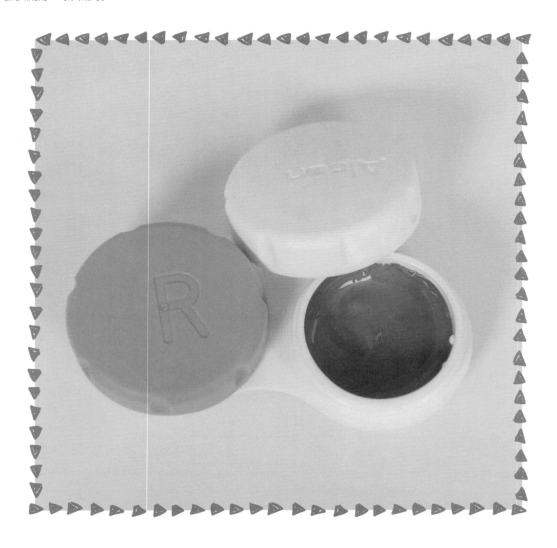

FOR A SHORT TRIP, STORE YOUR LIQUID PRODUCTS, SUCH AS
FOUNDATION OR EYE CREAM, IN A CONTACT LENS CASE.

NEED A GAME FOR OVER-ENTHUSIASTIC KIDS?
DICE IN A TRANSPARENT CUP WITH A LID WILL NEVER GET OLD.

A SOUVENIR FROM "DOUCE FRANCE"? PACK THE WINE
BOTTLE INSIDE A CHILD'S INFLATED FLOTATION DEVICE.

TIE A FLASHY SCARF AROUND YOUR SUITCASE—YOU'LL NEVER
HAVE TO LOOK FOR YOUR OWN LUGGAGE!

AVOID THE NAGGING "ARE WE THERE YET?" WITH THIS SMART TIP.
HANG A RIBBON FROM LEFT TO RIGHT BETWEEN THE TWO FRONT
SEATS, DIVIDED IN SECTIONS FOR EACH HOUR OF THE TRIP. MAKE
A PAPER CAR AND SLIDE THE CAR FORWARD EVERY HOUR.

DO YOU ALWAYS FORGET WHICH SIDE OF THE CAR THE GAS TANK
IS ON? PRO TIP: IN MOST CARS, THERE'S A LITTLE ARROW NEXT TO
THE FUEL GAUGE, SHOWING YOU ON WHICH SIDE YOU CAN FILL UP.

PENNY IN YO' PANTS: RIDE A BICYCLE WEARING A DRESS, WITHOUT FLASHING! HOLD A COIN AT THE BOTTOM FRONT OF YOUR DRESS AND TURN IT. FASTEN WITH A RUBBER BAND.

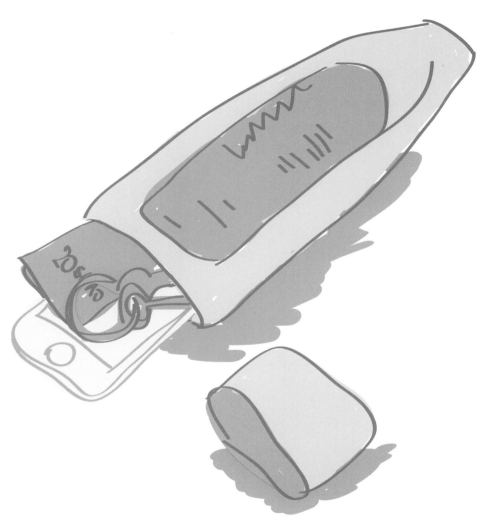

HIDE YOUR VALUABLES—MONEY, KEYS, CREDIT CARDS—ON
THE BEACH IN AN EMPTY SUNSCREEN BOTTLE. GOLDEN TIP!
(UNLESS THIEVES ARE READING THIS BOOK, OF COURSE.)

© 2015 UITGEVERIJ LANNOO NV. FOR THE ORIGINAL EDITION.
ORIGINAL TITLE: LIFE HACKS. TRANSLATED FROM THE DUTCH LANGUAGE.
WWW.LANNOO.COM

© 2016 WELDON OWEN INC. FOR THE ENGLISH EDITION.

ENGLISH TRANSLATION BY MARGUERITE STORM.

ALL RIGHTS RESERVED, INCLUDING THE RIGHT OF REPRODUCTION
IN WHOLE OR IN PART IN ANY FORM.

WELDON OWEN IS A DIVISION OF BONNIER PUBLISHING.
1045 SANSOME STREET, SUITE 100
SAN FRANCISCO, CA 94111
WWW.WELDONOWEN.COM

LIBRARY OF CONGRESS CATALOGING-IN-PUBLICATION DATA IS AVAILABLE.

THIS EDITION PRINTED IN 2016
10 9 8 7 6 5 4 3 2 1

ISBN 13: 978-1-68188-112-6
ISBN 10: 1-68188-112-8

PRINTED IN CHINA BY 1010 PRINTING.

TEXT   SARAH DEVOS
PHOTOGRAPHY   ANN DE KOKER (EXCEPT FOR P. 117, 129, AND 156)
PHOTOGRAPHY FOR P. 117, 129, AND 156   RACHEL LOPEZ METZGER
ILLUSTRATION   VALÉRIE MACHTELINCKX